LEGO

BY ALEXANDER LOWE

NORWOODHOUSE PRESS

Norwood House Press

For information regarding Norwood House Press, please visit our website at www.norwoodhousepress.com or call 866-565-2900.

Credits
Editor: Lauren Dupuis-Perez
Designer: Sara Radka
Fact Checker: Leah Kaminski and Renae Gilles
Special thanks to Wendy Vogelgesang.

Photo Credits
Flickr: Brickset, 41, ICONNA/Glòria Sánchez, 29, wiredforlego, 13; Getty Images: Donna Ward, 21, Ekaterina79, 15, Hulton Archive/Keystone/Kent Gavin, 7, Imeh Akpanudosen, 19, Kevork Djansezian, 5, LEGO Education/FIRST/Brendon Thorne, 25, LEGO/Tristan Fewings, 17, Oli Scarff, 23, Thierry Chesnot, 20, Tim P. Whitby, 9, Win McNamee, 26; Pixabay: aitoff, 10, 11, 16, 27, 36, andraberila, 37, blickpixel, 22, 31, Efraimstochter, 39, FelixMittermeier, 43, Legobibel, 4, MAKY_OREL, 12, Regenwolke, 3, sonlandras, 35; Shutterstock: 1000 Words Photos, cover, 1, Joaquin Corbalan P, 40; Wikimedia: Biswarup Ganguly, 30, TECHNIK BEGEISTERT e.V., 32

Library of Congress Cataloging-in-Publication Data
Names: Lowe, Alexander, author.
Title: Lego / by Alexander Lowe.
Description: Chicago : Norwood House Press, 2020. | Series: A great game! | Includes index. | Audience: Ages 8-10 | Audience: Grades 4-6 | Summary: "An introductory look at LEGO. Describes the history of the product, introduces the creators and innovators, highlights competitions, and provides insight about the company's future. Informational text for readers who are new to LEGO, or are interested in learning more. Includes a glossary, index, and bibliography for further reading"—Provided by publisher.
Identifiers: LCCN 2020019466 (print) | LCCN 2020019467 (ebook) | ISBN 9781684508525 (hardcover) | ISBN 9781684046003 (paperback) | ISBN 9781684046041 (epub)
Subjects: LCSH: LEGO toys.
Classification: LCC TS2301.T7 L68 2020 (print) | LCC TS2301.T7 (ebook) | DDC 688.7/25—dc23
LC record available at https://lccn.loc.gov/2020019466
LC ebook record available at https://lccn.loc.gov/2020019467

Hardcover ISBN: 978-1-68450-852-5
Paperback ISBN: 978-1-68404-600-3

LEGO™ is a registered trademark of LEGO KIRKBI A/S.
This book is not associated with LEGO™, Kirkbi A/S, or the LEGO Foundation.

328N—072020
Manufactured in the United States of America in North Mankato, Minnesota.

Table of Contents

A Visit to the Castle

A walkway leads to a huge castle. Its arched doorway is surrounded by two tall towers. Colorful flags hang from the towers. Knights in shiny armor guard the entrance.

There are hundreds of rooms inside the castle. A green dragon is perched on a balcony overlooking the lobby. Brightly colored bedrooms are fit for kings and queens. There are dining areas with tables ready for a royal feast.

This may seem like a scene from a fairy tale. But the walkway, towers, and rooms inside this castle are part of the LEGOLAND Castle Hotel in California. The hotel looks like it was built from giant LEGO blocks. Visitors can imagine themselves as tiny figures inside of a huge LEGO playset.

History of LEGO

The company that became LEGO began in 1932 in Billund, Denmark. The founder's name was Ole Kirk Christiansen. He was a carpenter. He made wooden ladders, ironing boards, and toys. Christiansen named his company LEGO in 1934. The word LEGO comes from the Danish phrase *leg godt*. It means "play well." One of Christiansen's first well-known toys was a wooden duck. LEGO started having money problems. Christiansen decided to only make toys. This helped the company. LEGO was making more than 40 different toys by 1936.

By 1949, LEGO was making around 200 different toys. Building blocks were one of the most popular. The company began making self-locking blocks in 1949. They were called "Automatic Binding Bricks." These were an early type of today's LEGO bricks.

DID YOU KNOW?

There is debate over what to call the famous bricks. Some people say LEGOs. But the LEGO company insists it is LEGO, no matter how many you have!

Children have been playing with LEGO for many years.

LEGO took a big step in 1953. They changed the name of their blocks. "Automatic Binding Bricks" became "LEGO." LEGO was selling 28 different playsets by 1955. They also sold eight toy vehicles. The company got a **patent** in 1958. It was for the stud-and-tube block connection system. Today's LEGO bricks are known for this system.

The bricks sold today came out in 1963. LEGO started using a special kind of plastic that year. It is still used to make the bricks. From here, the company started to expand and create theme parks. The first LEGOLAND opened in 1968. It was in Billund, Denmark. About 625,000 people went to the theme park the first season. There are now 10 LEGOLAND Parks. They are located around the world. Around 15.6 million people visited the parks in 2018. LEGOLAND Parks have many rides and activities. They are based on LEGO bricks and themes.

DID YOU KNOW?

One of LEGO's newest theme parks is located about 60 miles (97 kilometers) north of New York City. One of its seven themed areas is a LEGO factory where visitors experience how LEGO bricks are made from the perspective of a minifigure.

A model of Windsor Castle was put on permanent display at LEGOLAND in England to celebrate the 2018 wedding of Prince Harry and Meghan Markle.

History of LEGO: Time Line

1932
Ole Kirk Christiansen starts making wooden toys in his shop in Billund, Denmark.

1958
LEGO patents the stud-and-tube block, which remains unchanged for the next 60 years.

1968
The first LEGOLAND theme park opens in Billund, Denmark, and features detailed city scenes.

1978
LEGO releases its first minifigures with movable arms and legs.

1998
LEGO releases programmable robotic LEGO sets called Mindstorms, which are the basis for FIRST LEGO League competitions around the world.

2014
The LEGO Movie premiers and is an immediate success. The movie leads to increased sales in LEGO toys around the world.

2020
After three years of development, LEGO releases Braille bricks for visually impaired users.

LEGO began selling around the world in the 1960s. They were sold in many countries outside of Denmark. The first new countries were in Europe. Stores in the United States and Canada started selling them too. Twelve years later, offices then opened in the United States. LEGO bricks are now sold in more than 140 countries.

One well-known part of LEGO sets is the minifigures. The first ones were sold in 1978. They had movable arms and legs. This made creating themed sets possible. LEGO made themed sets based on castles, pirates, and space. They also made sets based on popular cartoons, movies, and books.

Happy Birthday, Bricks

LEGO bricks turned 60 years old in 2018. The stud-and-tube system was patented in 1958. This made the toys more durable. It is the foundation that the company is still based on. The bricks were made of new plastic in the 1960s. This made them even stronger. Bricks from the 1960s do not look much different than bricks made today. The system is the same. New bricks can be used with any bricks from 1958 or later.

LEGO blocks are one of the most successful toys of all time. New products have helped the company stay competitive. LEGO joined the digital world with Mindstorms toys in 1998. The company released its first blockbuster film, *The LEGO Movie*, in 2014. In 2020, Braille Bricks made LEGO accessible to visually impaired users. LEGO keeps finding ways to appeal to new fans.

DID YOU KNOW?

Ole Kirk Christiansen's son Godtfred started working in his father's shop when he was just 12 years old.

All in the Family

LEGO has been around for more than 85 years. It is still a family-owned and family-operated business. Ole Kirk Christiansen ran the company when it started. His son Godtfred took over the company after his father retired in 1956. He was involved until 1995. His son, Kjeld Kirk Kristiansen, was next. He became the president and CEO of the LEGO Group in 1979. He was elected into the Toy Industry Hall of Fame in 2008. His grandfather also holds this honor.

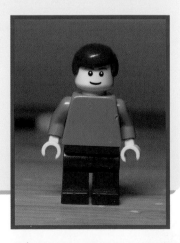

LEGOLAND Parks are one way LEGO appeals to a wider audience. Families and people of all ages can enjoy LEGO when they visit one of the parks.

LEGO Basics

Ole Kirk Christiansen made the first LEGO toys by hand in his workshop. LEGO started making plastic toys in 1946. They used a plastic injection molding machine. This machine heats plastic and then pours it into a mold, or hollow shape. The plastic hardens and forms in the shape of the mold. Although LEGO are still made this way, the process for coming up with new LEGO ideas is very different.

DID YOU KNOW?

LEGO opened its first private school in Denmark in 2013. Children who attend the school are given a lot of freedom. They can explore their creative sides and be young inventors.

The original LEGO minifigures have evolved to include more looks and styles than the original, basic yellow man.

There is a designer for every new set or minifigure. Sometimes a whole team works on one new set. LEGO designers are paid to build with LEGO all day. Some might make giant **replicas** of superheroes. Others help create new rides for LEGOLAND. These artists have many backgrounds. Most study 3D arts. Others are **industrial** designers or **architects**. Some are even carpenters like Ole Kirk Christiansen. One thing is for sure, all designers must have a good imagination.

Materials

LEGO bricks are made from a plastic known as ABS. This material has many benefits. It is very strong and durable. Its color also resists fading better than most plastics. ABS turns to liquid when heated, so it is ideal for LEGO's injection molding process. The plastic is heated to 450 degrees Fahrenheit (232 degrees Celsius) and then molded into LEGO bricks. The plastic is kept in big **silos**. LEGO plants have around 14 silos that hold a total of 33 tons (30 metric tons) of plastic.

LEGO launched a campaign called Rebuild the World in 2019 to encourage people to think outside the box when building with LEGO blocks. The campaign includes programs on social media and live LEGO building events.

There is also a Future Lab at LEGO. This team helps keep the toy company ahead of the times. The Future Lab comes up with creative ways to play with LEGO. These include **apps** and internet games. In 2003, LEGO sales were down and they were in debt. Designers did research. They looked at what fans were buying and how they played with LEGO blocks. They found out what people wanted to buy. They created movies, TV shows, and games based on LEGO. Their efforts paid off. The Future Lab helped LEGO become popular again. In 2017, the company was named the world's most powerful brand by *Forbes* magazine.

The *LEGO Movie* was released in 2014. The company made more than 15 new playsets based on the movie. The *LEGO Batman Movie* and *LEGO Movie 2: The Second Part* were also popular. The LEGO movies were made to look similar to **stop-motion animation**. Many fans enjoy making short stop-motion animation films with LEGO bricks and posting them online. The filmmakers wanted to honor this fan hobby. The *Ninjago* TV series has been on since 2011. *Ninjago* combines LEGO and ninjas. Kids loved the movies and shows. It made them interested in building with LEGO bricks.

The LEGO Movie premiered in Los Angeles on February 1, 2014. Life-size LEGO minifigures were on hand to celebrate with fans.

Nathan Sawaya's 2018 traveling art show included DC superheroes made of LEGO bricks.

By 2016, LEGO was selling 75 billion bricks per year. There were more minifigures on Earth than people. The company was more successful than it had been in years. The movies and television shows led to new interest in LEGO. The company needed a leader who understood the ever-changing world of toys.

LEGO named a new **CEO** in 2017. It was Niels B. Christiansen. He was a very successful businessman. Christiansen wanted to work at LEGO. He loves LEGO. "I have loved building with LEGO bricks since I was a child," Christiansen said.

The Art of the Brick

Nathan Sawaya had a good life. He was a corporate lawyer in New York City. But he had another passion. He loved building with LEGO. He quit his job to design unique LEGO artwork. Sawaya's traveling art show has broken attendance records at galleries around the world. It is called "The Art of the Brick." His work has been called one of the world's "must-see exhibitions." Sawaya uses LEGO to make all the artwork.

Many toy companies have struggled in recent years. But Christiansen thinks LEGO can stay on top. **Technology** can help. Christiansen wants to use technology to make LEGO better. Many kids today have tablets and smartphones. Christiansen wants to connect those devices to LEGO bricks. This gives kids more options for building with LEGO bricks. But even with advances in technology, the simple design of LEGO blocks has not changed. Kids have to build objects like cars or robots before they can connect them to apps or games. This sets LEGO apart from other toys and helps the company stay true to its simple roots.

DID YOU KNOW?

Students at a college in China can take classes in LEGO building. Teachers see the classes as a way to develop innovators and designers.

LEGO Mindstorms EV3 robots were one of 2013's top tech toys. Users control them using an app on a phone or tablet.

LEGO Competitions

Most people build with LEGO for fun. But many LEGO products are also used in schools. LEGO products, such as Mindstorms EV3, teach kids how to solve problems. These special sets include programmable bricks, motors, sensors, cables, and LEGO Technic elements. There are also LEGO competitions. These are events where people play against each other. They are for students in elementary through high school.

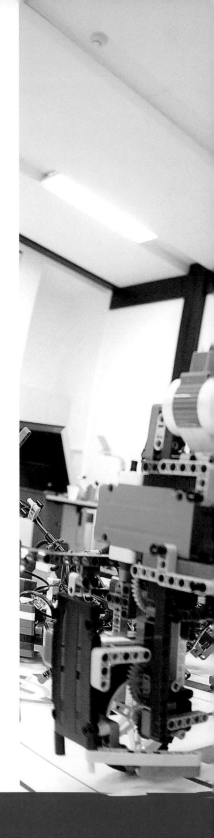

DID YOU KNOW?

Thousands of LEGO fans travel to BrickUniverse every year. These LEGO fan conventions are held all over the world. A 14-year-old builder named Greyson Beights started BrickUniverse in 2015.

FIRST LEGO League events are held in many countries around the world each year.

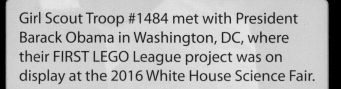

Girl Scout Troop #1484 met with President Barack Obama in Washington, DC, where their FIRST LEGO League project was on display at the 2016 White House Science Fair.

The FIRST LEGO League is one competition. It started in 1998 as a test program. It became an official contest in 1999. There were 960 teams that year. FIRST LEGO League combines LEGO with robots. The event is held at different places in the United States. There are also events around the world.

Record-Breaking Bricks

Guinness World Records keeps track of many LEGO records. Some LEGO collections have set world records. The most valuable LEGO minifigure is a gold version of Boba Fett from *Star Wars*. It is worth more than $11,000. The largest collection of minifigures belongs to an Italian man. He owns 3,310. The largest collection of LEGO sets is 3,837. It is owned by an Australian man. That collection has more than 1.2 million individual bricks. It also has more than 8,000 LEGO minifigures.

Students do real-world science challenges in FIRST LEGO League. They also solve technology problems. FIRST LEGO League is for students ages 9 to 16. Students get hands-on STEM experiences. STEM stands for science, technology, engineering, and math. Students also gain confidence. They develop habits of learning. The coaches encourage students to try many things. Failing is okay. Trying is what is important.

There are also LEGO events for younger students. FIRST LEGO League Jr. is for children ages 6 to 10. Discovery Edition of FIRST LEGO League is for even younger students. They are in kindergarten and first grade.

FIRST LEGO League has different themes each year. Some include Animal Allies, Into Orbit, City Shaper, and Food Factor. In 2018, more than 300,000 students competed.

FIRST LEGO participants often take engineering classes their first year in college. They are 2.6 times more likely to do this. More than 75 percent of former competitors are studying or working in a STEM job.

DID YOU KNOW?

The top 20 FIRST LEGO League semi-finalist teams compete for the Global Innovation Award, which provides the winning team with a $20,000 prize.

FIRST LEGO League now gives a total of 14 or more awards depending on the competition.

The Indian National Championship of the World Robot Olympiad 2016 was held at Netaji Indoor Stadium in Calcutta, India.

The World Robot Olympiad (WRO) works with LEGO Education. They host other LEGO contests. The WRO LEGO contests are for kids through young adults. Participants range from elementary school through age 25. Teams have two or three members. Each team has one coach. They design, build, and program a robot. The robot must solve a problem. Points are earned for completing a list of tasks. LEGO Mindstorms and other LEGO parts are used for the event.

Brick Tube

One of the most popular ways LEGO fans share their passion is through YouTube. There are many LEGO channels. People post how-to videos and reviews. Some film creative uses for existing LEGO sets. These are called **hack** videos. They have been viewed hundreds of millions of times. There are LEGO accounts on Instagram. Some have tens of thousands of followers. One of the most popular is "legojacker." That account shows pictures of LEGO minifigures placed all over the world.

The football category at WRO can be as exciting as a real football match for some LEGO fans.

One WRO LEGO contest is a football tournament. Football is another word for soccer. There is only one age group for this competition. Everyone ages 10 to 19 plays against each other. The teams use LEGO bricks and a motor. Each team builds two robots. Then the tournament begins. The robots play a game of soccer against another team's robots. This is a fun way to combine LEGO with other interests.

Like the FIRST LEGO League, the WRO has big goals for their competitions. There were just over 26,000 teams from 68 countries in the 2018 WRO competition. In the future, they hope to involve kids from every country around the world. They want to make sure kids from every background have access to robotics and STEM programs.

DID YOU KNOW?

A 9-year-old girl from London is the youngest LEGO designer. She designed a playground as part of a 2017 LEGO Friends Designer Competition. Her design even had a minifigure of herself. LEGO created her design and sold it in stores.

Future of LEGO

Themed sets are some of LEGO's best-selling products. There are many different themes. LEGO has made sets based on Minecraft, superheroes, and Disney Princesses. Themed sets are fun because they can match a player with their personal interests, whether its movies, TV shows, careers, construction, or some other hobby.

DID YOU KNOW?

LEGO produces around 2.16 million bricks per hour, or about 36,000 per minute!

Playing with LEGO can be an introduction to many different career opportunities for young children.

Many toys are moving to digital platforms, but building with LEGO bricks can offer a form of play that does not require computers.

There are even themed sets geared toward adults. Some of these sets are complex. Many have thousands of small pieces. LEGO has tried to appeal to many interests. In 2019, the company released a set based on the TV show *Friends*. They also released a set based on the show *Stranger Things*. There are models of expensive cars. Other sets look like city skylines. There is also a series of NASA spaceships. Some of these sets are very expensive.

Plant-Based Plastic

Plastic products create a concern for the environment. Plastic does not break down quickly. It can lead to pollution. Many people worry about the effects of plastic on the planet. LEGO has responded with an innovative idea. In 2018, the company produced its first bricks made of plant-based materials. Finding the proper material has been challenging. LEGO wants to create a durable product in a **sustainable** way. The company wants to make all their products from sustainable sources. They have set a goal to do this by the year 2030.

LEGO also makes sets for much younger children. These are called DUPLO. The company has been making DUPLO blocks since 1969. The blocks are much larger than traditional LEGO. DUPLO blocks come in different shapes and colors to help small children learn. There are blocks for children as young as 1 year old.

The company has also branched into the **digital** world. Around 50 million people use LEGO's social media pages each month. LEGO also has an online ideas page. At this website, the company takes suggestions for new products. Different contests are posted. Fans can share their ideas. Other LEGO fans can vote on their favorites. Some of the contests get hundreds of entries. Winning ideas might be made into a real LEGO product. Fans are designing toys they might someday buy.

DID YOU KNOW?

LEGO bricks have been to space! U.S. astronauts took LEGO sets to the International Space Station in 2011. They built objects using LEGO bricks with kids who were watching on Earth. The students got to see firsthand what it would be like to build with LEGO bricks without gravity!

DUPLO bricks are easier for small children to play with and feature themes that help younger users learn about the world around them.

LEGO WeDo 2.0 is an app that allows kids to build and code robots and other machines using LEGO bricks and programmable sensors.

LEGO uses technology in other ways too. There are more than 20 LEGO apps for phones and tablets. One app is called LEGO Tower. The game lets users build skyscrapers with **virtual** bricks. They collect minifigures, vehicles, and other objects. Users can even visit other players' towers in the game.

Braille Bricks

In 2017, LEGO began to work with the blind. They released LEGO Braille Bricks in 2020. These bricks can help blind children learn to read. The bricks include letters in the Braille alphabet. They also work with other LEGO sets.

The company has found other ways to use digital apps. One new project is called LEGO Hidden Side. These are special LEGO sets. Kids can use a smartphone app with a physical brick set. The app is an **augmented reality** (AR) game. This means that it combines the blocks in the real world with an app. The game features haunted places, such as buildings and graveyards. With the AR app, the places become more than just LEGO sets. Users can hunt and trap ghosts. They can play alone or with friends. A team worked on the Hidden Side. It took more than a year. Then about 1,400 families tested the app.

Apps and games give users new ways to play with one of the world's simplest toys. LEGO has connected with new users through technology without replacing the most important part of their product, the stud-and-tube block. Today's LEGO builders have many choices. They can make their LEGO robot come to life. They can use an app to interact with their blocks. Or they can build a scene from scratch like their parents and grandparents did many years ago. The possibilities are endless.

LEGO products like Technic sets combine simple blocks with special gears, pins, and axles. Some even include small motors.

Glossary

apps: programs or games made for tablets or smartphones

architects: people who design buildings

augmented reality: adding objects, such as buildings or animals, to the real world using a computer or other device

CEO: chief executive officer, the person in charge of a company

digital: relating to television, computers, social media, and other types of media

hack: finding a different use for something or using an object in an unusual way

industrial: relating to factories and the field of manufacturing

patent: exclusive right granted by the government to make an item

replicas: exact copies of something

silos: large towers used for storage

stop-motion animation: style of filmmaking in which a series of pictures is taken of objects in slightly different positions so they look like they are moving

sustainable: long-lasting

technology: the invention of new ways of doing something

virtual: something that appears real but cannot be touched

For More Information

Books

Hugo, Simon. *356 Things to Do with LEGO Bricks: LEGO Fun Every Day of the Year.* London: DK Children, 2016. This book features new ways to play with traditional LEGO bricks. From stop-motion video ideas to building challenges, discover a unique LEGO activity for every day of the year.

Lipkowitz, Daniel. *The LEGO Book.* New York: DK Publishing, 2018. This book covers everything LEGO, from how the bricks are made to how you can use them to create amazing masterpieces. Learn more about the various franchises that have partnered with LEGO, including Star Wars and Marvel Comics, and discover secret tricks and tips from LEGO Master Builders.

Websites

The Best Kids LEGO Activities (https://littlebinsforlittlehands.com/kids-lego-activities/) This article includes more than 100 experiments, activities, and fun ideas using LEGO bricks for kids of all ages.

LEGO Kids Experience. (https://www.lego.com/en-us/kids) This website especially for kids includes the latest news about LEGO products, how-to videos, games, and updates about the newest LEGO themed building sets.

Index

About the Author

Alexander Lowe is a writer who splits his time between Los Angeles and Chicago. He has written children's books about sports, technology, science, and media. He has also done extensive work as a sportswriter and film critic. He loves reading books of any and all kinds.